HAWAI'I POEMS
from there to here

Pianta

Copyright © 2020 by Pianta. All rights reserved. No part of this publication may be reproduced, distributed, or transmitted in any form or by any means, including photocopying, recording, or other electronic or mechanical methods, without the prior written permission of the publisher, except in the case of brief quotations embodied in critical reviews and certain other noncommercial uses permitted by copyright law.

HAWAI‘I POEMS from there to here
Pianta

TABLE OF CONTENTS
Preface
Section One
- Reckless 11
- Territory 12
- Consolation 14
- Atrium 16
- The Summer You Knew Me 17
- August 18
- Tusitala 19
- Mango 22
- Orange Juice 24
- Day of Colored Bangles 26
- Water and Sky 28

Section Two
- Rain Poems 32
- Baban and Her Senkkoo 34
- Ojiichan 36
- Mother 38
- Father 40
- You Walk Out to the Water 42
- How I See Him 43
- Jinzhan Yintai 44
- Spring 45
- Compass 46
- And Wind I Heard 48
- In the Quiet There Is A Distance 54

Section Three
> Ethnobotany 59
> The Essential Nature of Things 60
> Land of Obligation 62
> The Ideal Man 67
> This Time 68
> Hāpu‘u 70

Acknowledgments 73
Publication credits 76

PREFACE

Even though I think of these as "Hawai'i" poems, every poem I write feels like it has its roots in Hawai'i. I wrote many of them a long time ago, but they continue to mean a lot to me, and I wanted to put them together in a collection. While some of them were published previously, others are being published for the first time. They are grouped in sections but are not in chronological order. They include some of the first poems I've written and others that I've just finished. The poems reflect the many changes I've experienced as a writer and as a person. For that reason, rather than rework the poems to reflect one style or format, I've tried to keep them as close to the original versions as possible.

Lastly, Hawai'i has a powerful, unmistakable presence. I hope some of its influence can be felt in these pieces.

Section One

RECKLESS

You fell so far, so deep. You could no longer feel the edges of your body. The weather he felt, you felt. The thoughts he ran from, you saw. The dreams he had, you woke with. The commitments he made to others, you helped him keep.

When you fought, the moon faded, the continents began to shift, the rains started, and the animals shrank in fear.

You parted.

So you find yourself in a very quiet place. In this devastation of the heart, you push away the grief, the burdens, the floods. You push off whatever you know of him onto the small paper boats that are shoved from the banks with sparks from votives that fly into cool lunar evenings, and you wonder how those cinders can make it because they're held only by boats that shift easily in the wind.

And even though your heart is breaking, and your arrogance and recklessness are faltering, you let him go, let him go, let him go. And later, inside yourself, you don't know how deep you were in this water, or how long you could have survived without air, or how you ever got yourself back to shore.

TERRITORY

he lured me from agoraphobia
and took me where I couldn't go alone
but now I am strangled by the vines of his thoughts
that still wrap themselves around mine

I play music so loudly
that it penetrates the fiber of the walls

I tidy papers and mail letters that say curtly
"I am tired of speaking of failure"

I rearrange my cats
and encourage them to sleep some place that is different

this is a team effort

we are all in unfamiliar territory
places where we can no longer get white chalk
and mark big thick lines
telling ourselves we are safe as long as we stay here

CONSOLATION

such a heart those bodies must carry
lit from inside
their polished eyes
submerged black pearls

they have larger brains than humans
though it is not so much the brain
but the heart I wonder about

the way they swim together
gliding along whales
nosing their way through water
surrounded by a watery aquamarine
so different from the soft dust
their predecessors dragged their bellies on

this is a cold city, I think, as I drive the freeway paths
the organs of my body
plated with the grief of occasions
I choose not to talk about

once I mourned a friend
but couldn't stop

locked in a car on the freeway
like a sterling silver jewelry box
careening down a fatal staircase

I held my thoughts inside
as gently as pearls held within the lips of a shell

and I headed toward the sea

my heart's not big enough
to exist in the ocean as they do

free to let their limbs move in the lovely pressure of water
forming them without and within

my own brain sits cradled on shoulders
burdened by all the things I don't know
and worse, by the things I don't care about

not caring is another death
another step taken away from the water

on the way home

I look outward
the sky has lit up

streetlights are
flying fish
moving across a thick plate of glass

ATRIUM

I twist in the blue saline that holds me afloat
and there are only two things I know:
the heavens made the waters and they made you

this I consider under a sky as bright as a movie screen
with palms backlit
as green as avocado skins
and I let the words you say
drift on my skin like frail, invisible tattoos
as clear as the membranes of jellyfish
that leave red, bitter welts that I do not yet feel

and your words have fallen
hundreds of feet
in the shape of blossoms
drifting as they did from the balcony
where we stood in the dark
drifting into the atrium
where the sun today soars and peaks
leaving slashes of light
on my arms and legs
leading me to be sea

THE SUMMER YOU KNEW ME

every color here is clear
true to its origins
mangoes ripen true green true red true yellow

babies sway
milk and shade honoring them
drowsiness overlapping the heat

I felt this way when I loved him
like a body of petals
uncurling to the motion of touch

in the heat of summer
fists release
muscles ease themselves in water
ailments fade
bruises lose purple
and legs slide
beneath thin airy sheets

all forms of heat merely variations of love

AUGUST

I was wearing thin muslin
bothered by mosquitos
that bit through to my skin
but I was settled with music you played

strange chords I hadn't heard before

your wrist struck the keys with such defiance

that night I thought of you and walked home alone
white clouds trailed across the Ko'olaus
as quickly as a girl running through a field

but all I could do
was make my way back slowly
past the wild orchids that hung, bobbing
as if they heard the notes in the damp air

I couldn't sleep
after a night filled with such music
and only now can write this
on a plane to you

TUSITALA

the light draws slats across your face as you walk
among the giant leaves and dropped pods

they're so brittle that they crack as you walk over them
you hold one up
and light from the moon comes through pinholes
that the worms have eaten through

the wet from dew and showers
Mānoa does liberally over you as you make your way
among the elephant ear

we pass where Tusitala once stayed
surrounded by monstera with midribs so thick
the juncture of the leaf to stem is formidable
they are as broad as your open, spread hands
the hands that strike against my wrist
to show me the action one needs to play your music

you say you hear tones when you go up past Hillside
gesturing, you pass the corner with the clusters
of spider lily and your shoulder bumps
their narrow tubes with sticky clear dew

they catch streetlight like stars
but you don't notice
you keep walking

your hands and fingers gesticulating
like a dalang master
making shadows into puppets at the moon

MANGO

my brother reaches up to pick the mango
but is it ripe?

all of us pass the teaspoon
to taste the mango sauce that Sue made

it's a refinement of mango
a conversion of fumes that return to the sun

it's a world of mangoes rolling on roads
of mango blossoms falling out of my hair

it's allergies and inhalers
that spar with mangoes crammed into freezers
golden fibrous ice caps
that wait for their end
in mango bread, chutney
or beyond the season, to be 86'd in the bin

we cast lines for the mango fish
with poles that get tangled in the trees
while leaves as crisp as potato chips
float down the stream

ORANGE JUICE

things that have finger texture—
a leaf, a blade of grass,
the underbelly of a puppy,
mapped with birthmarks like small continents—

these come through the eyes funnel
through the pores of the body funnel
and keep moving through the skinny passageway

they pass through in miniature
then emerge and enlarge inside

Delaina has a new juice strainer

on the day it was brand new
we took it to the beach and squeezed 18 oranges
for a vitamin C charge

we sat in the wind and sand
and squeezed oranges with this—
the yellow plastic strainer with white cup and handle

a squeezer, a cup, a handle for easy pouring—
how flexible!

a utensil of such dimension!

in dimensions unknown to eyes
atoms form architectural wonders
many stories high
of tetrahedron, double tetrahedron,
stacks of slippery magazines that somehow stay

the juice that enters our mouths
recrystallizes into vitamins
the orange colored energy reconverted
to arms and legs
moving in long strides down the beach

DAY OF COLORED BANGLES

1.
this morning I had four colored bangles on
one orange, one yellow, one white, and one green

they made a zinging sound
as they rolled up and down my arm
they are thin metal hoops
like the five silver rings of the magician—
the ones that are connected and then they are apart

the sun is a golden hoop around a rim that separates
into a three-ring circus

yellow diamond sewn to orange diamond to white to green
clowns wear these costumes
with Elizabethan collars of white honeycombs

they have carrot-shredded hair
and they do cartwheels around the world

2.
a colored-wire lotus from a novelty shop folds like a puzzle
a house has a porch railing like arching rainbows

the world is a place of brightly colored arcs
arcs are half hoops

hoops run down hills into shrubs into yards
kids push tires on a swing

3.

I used to have a fluorescent pink hula hoop
I would run, whip that hoop around and rotate

we'd stand in a centrifugal force symphony:
six kids in hula hoops
there, in our Palolo house garage,
we'd eat orange ice cake

we'd hit the ice with our forks,
leaving pools of orange on the floor
then somebody would roll out their hoop
and we'd chase it, laughing,
and a car would come down the driveway
and bend it in half!

4.

hoops of the world, rims of the universe, wobbling,
making liquid figure eights, picking up speed,
like a skater, a turn,
saving the best for last,
the last whoosh, the last zing, the last flash
of the hula hoop-universe dance

WATER AND SKY

silk is pulled
over the already drowsy planet
and humans move more slowly
under this apricot colored sky

the unwinding of the day has begun

the night begins to seep in
and islands bow to the grace of this moment

palms drape fronds over themselves
as gracefully as women retreating modestly for the night

the air changes
and horses nuzzle the moisture of the sea left on leaves

dampness starts to stain the sky
as inevitably as ink to paper
indigo mixed with striations of the sun

I shower
and my slightly burnt skin is hesitant to water
my black hair full
nearly to the waist
adheres to the lines of my body

wavering
in the water currents
and I wring it and coil it
black tassel of silk
as that hot orange ball sets in the window

SECTION TWO

RAIN POEMS

1.
rain hits the street like a million spiders
scrambling for holes
and the mynah stands
chirping as drops run off his back
on the lava wall

cars swish by

rust spots grow
like small wildflowers
on the railing of this bus stop

2.
raindrops beat on giant ferns

they are enormous elephant ears
delicately fluttering

the forest is deep

beetles crawl on the underside of dirt clods
and banyan roots
toppling side to side when hit by long tear-shaped drops

they free fall
stick to a slender green branch and slide down

they hit a dusty beetle
until the blackness of the beetle is wet and polished

everything
is quiet

BABAN AND HER SENKOO

a thin black stick of incense makes a smoke tail
that wavers and flicks
like the fine gold carvings on the altar,
curling and weaving like the gnarls on Baban's hands,
hands that make green shrubs shoot out of the ground

her voice putters as she stands before the altar,
breathing in short bits of air like sips of water,
hands together, head bowed
she putters
like water over pebbles
at the mouth of a stream

OJIICHAN

1.
Ojiichan, I see you with your samisen
sitting in the dining room on the old plastic chair

when you played the samisen, your lips barely moved

when I climbed onto your lap, you would smile, wordless

your face hardly moved, but it was like rock walls setting,
like the physical weathering of the valley behind our house

there were so many lines that cut into your face
and you were a strong man

Daddy said once that he would make money as you did
cutting and carrying cane in bundles
from the roadside to the trucks

it was money, so good money for those days
but you scolded him and said labor was hard
and without gratitude

2.
the ceremony when you were gone—
bright gold and orange colors on the altar
flowers thick on wreaths and on stands
nishime and kanten on platters on folding tables
kids running in circles in patent leather shoes

Baban's friends chanting:
women's voices moving up and down stairs
and the gong making waves we would nod to

we stood outside, fitting onto the steps
in black and white faces
the camera beginning at one end
slowly turning
all of us motionless, waiting for the exposure
without smiles

3.
I knew I loved you then, Jiichan
but where were the words?
I didn't have all the time in the world
and yet you knew me, "Shoori," small chawan-cut girl

I hope you remember me on your lap, holding tight

this has been returned to me
the altar in my heart
where I place tangerines and fresh chrysanthemums
for your eyes and lips

it's there for you to sit and play your samisen
from sunrise to sunset
you, making music
as I sit and close my eyes

MOTHER

my mother combed her hair in the reeds
and let it float on the water
    leaning her hair back
      she let the water seep into
          the fiber   her hair collected
                blue stars that would shine
          when she was happy
           she slept inside the hollow of the
tree
                in the morning shaking out her
              just washed hair and yellow leaf and flower
bits would catch on the ends of her
      hair and birds came by to nip at them
      to tease her
my mother fell in love with my father
    because she loved the daylight and she thought
        he would be a good guide to the night
           he would know the water night birds
and he could watch for night animals
  they would ride the bus
        around the island at night and
           find places to go dancing
            in magazines there were
              pictures of double-breasted suits and
          party dresses but they
      would come home early
because their parents didn't like the blackouts

with children riding vehicles in the streets
    she thought his face was beautiful
   and his motions still
     together they could seep up water
  through their veins and fly starward
 open palmed to gather all the
material to make the houses for
 their children
  despite the red sun
   white flag sky of December 7
    Pearl Harbor notwithstanding
     people running in the streets
my mother fell in love
 my father fell in love
  their children have grown into
   rare species
    rare sorts of color
    rare spirits
     from that holy white heart branch

FATHER

        he followed his own blue smoke
      walking carefully between the crisscrossed reeds
sometimes he'd crouch in the tall grass
and watch the sun come up
  he never quite understood the lack of elegance in his life
    he would just sit silently
          stacking matchbook covers or
              mounds of twigs and when
    people would ask him for advice
      he would pause
          turn his head slightly
              then shake his head
                  saying only two or three words—
        the girls loved it—
      they thought his silence
    was so measured
they thought his rough hands
and callouses were only a disguise
  to hide him from rich
    brocaded men who didn't understand
      how a laborer could have the mind
              of a philosopher king
    weary sometimes at night he'd find
      his favorite place by the river
          and listen to the mother duck and

ducklings sing their way across the
river   she was so beautiful
the white beneath the feathers
showed and she never stopped
not even when the white blossoms
bumped her side
only for a moment
and then she'd take her
little babies to the other side
meanwhile across the river
my mother sang
long songs about
the farmers coming here and
missing their wives
and the special fish
they could catch and fry only
on their island

YOU WALK OUT TO THE WATER

under the sagging screen door of clouds
  you walk out to the water
        salt encrusted, you study the stars and the tide
          and as the water embraces your legs,
    your feet, your hips
        you tumble into white water
  lacing your fingers
you hold tight to the net
     certain you'll catch
        this woman fish

HOW I SEE HIM

a soldier in an old silk screen, gold, a few shimmers left
    his mustache is thin,
            flying up like long sea branches
the night is cool
    the moon setting in the window
        a rumpled bed in the darkness
    he hears the gecko

I am a milk-skinned woman wrapped
    in gold encrusted gowns
  whose red lips smile in his direction
    I dream of a slender boat
    myself under
  a flower-splattered parasol
      V's floating from fingertips
        flowers ride on the ripples
on the other side of the pond, he catches the blossoms
    with his fingers
    and mosquitos hum among the algae
and the lilies
  his skin is pale, dark and moist are his lips,
    eyes with almond brown centers
        I tilt my head, I slant my eyes away
  he sees the bone of my wrist, the quiet turn of my head
    I sit cool, a petal among smells of the morning

JINZHAN YINTAI

fish scatter
and people desire

such is the influence of our moon

in the lull of tides
and the quiet of the narcissus
we yearn for the sudden shift
away from death and distance
toward the cataclysms of waking

eager for the contact of skin
and for the immersion of water

beneath this burning bridge

SPRING
    "Lady Guoguo and Her Sisters on an Outing"

in her innocence
Lady Guoguo rides

her horse's hooves
leaving delicate imprints
on fragrant grass

absorbed by this beauty
Zhang Xuan captures her
in the patina of a scroll
only to have Emperor Huizong
steal this for his own dream

elusive in her joy;
she'll soon surrender to the fate of Yang Guifei
and the An Rebellion

but for now,
caught in the splendor
of billowing silk
and the groomed coiffure of the horse's tail,
she witnesses the ascension of her sisters,
who, in their loveliness,
rival the emergence of spring

COMPASS

I found you somehow,
sitting in a circle of people
over bowls of shark fin soup
and thin shreds of bamboo shoots,
drinking Chinese tea

And like a compass that wobbles
its needle unsure
I barely eat among these people that I do not know;
yet my laughter at your words—
some of them cutting
some of them warm—
has left imprints
as big as the peonies painted on the restaurant walls,
some of them as large as cabbages,
others the size of men's fists,
and later, when I walk out
to follow your lead to the freeway,
I get lost in the dark
and I suddenly feel how cold it is
and how far I flew
outside myself
talking with you tonight

AND WIND I HEARD

1.
Turning the hair.
You turned my hair blue
almost cruelly
taking me out to a white moon
flat flat
a coin dropped into a river—
even that slides between branches and takes shape.
You made our faces as flat and as white as the moon
all the sadness rippled off
all the green leaves drew away like fishes
to settle, to sleep.
I grabbed your hand
as you lifted me to the stars
a pinwheel—our legs moving in the wind
fabric flapping around me.
I perch on a branch
you say you want to see me
a woman in the wind
nearest feminine thing to the moon
and I toss down leaves, laughing
watching the grasses bend and twist
fingers knotting and releasing the moon
turning knuckles in the wind.

2.
I drew "solo" in the cards.
I ran toward the city
then through a narrow alleyway,
stumbling on a child's bell.

I held it to my chest
I still felt it ringing
as silk petals dropped from the kanzashii.
You followed me—them—like kernels of corn.
You swept behind me
silver sword hidden in blue silk you said
I couldn't run as fast as the blades
of grass and you laughed
slicing my words
before they dropped from my lips.
The stars broke from the swiftness
of my tongue
but when you told me
that you'd gather the swords together
and leave that life for me to choose,
I wept.

The river grows pink from the silk of the obi.
How could you know?
I threw the mats down, running bent over
the *tabi* gathering mustard dust
like old men's eyes filling.
I knew that I had three seasons.
Three cups full.
Ume red water to drink.
They say it makes the heart grow stronger.
My heart can't be held in my kimono—
when I look into the water
I see the blood rush to my ears.

Grant me three wishes.
I cut out stars from fabric,

shook three dried leaves
and took the purple sash I had saved
and wrapped them under a rock.
I met you under the river rocks,
below them where the water tumbled
white marble doors.
I grasped the branch of the bamboo,
let it snap in my fingers as I watched
you come down the path carrying silk:
one green with yellow storks,
two with dancing girls,
and one gold obi.
You had them in a basket
cook this you said—
when you laughed all things flashed
white.

3.
Sew this you said,
gathering the blue yukata in your hand.
You shouldn't have run over the rocks.
The wind's too swift
and the water follows it crazily in the wind.
You lose the color in your eyes
and everything gets white around you.
I don't seem to know you
but I called you over the rocks.
I saw you below.
I threw my slippers—
a feeble gesture—
your neck moved
as if you remembered your duties—

but I'm not young enough to follow you.
I'm not swift enough
to meet you at the bottom near the river.
The paths are so overgrown
that I can't find my way.
I'm afraid of the blades
that I may have dropped there
while you run headlong
the red kimono trailing over the green
like a red dragon.
I hurled slippers at you
and you stopped mid track—
now here you are nursing
your white feet in tea water.
The meijiro don't fear you.
They steal rice from your bowl.
Why do you look at me that way?
I brought you golden combs when I was young.

4.
O Yasu—I am happy.
The meijiro have come again.
They are rice clippings flying in the wind.
Green flecks spin and catch my eyes.
Their breasts look like the rounded cups
you set out for me one night.
We had ceremonies to keep us company.
You unwrapped the gold hashi.
We drank tea from a persimmon pot.
Tonight I'll unbind my hair.
Remember it like the ocean.

You took me here when we were young.
I took you there—you turned my hair
blue.
You scattered stars.
White cups shattered at my feet.
You said this is how our life begins:
rice for hair that doesn't hunger
stars for feet that don't wander.
I lost my heart to you.
You courted me.
You feared I'd fly off on a sparrow's tail
that I would grow into the silk ball on the fabric
that I would curl into the water
that wrapped itself against the rocks.
Shoji—I slide them shut as you sleep.
Looking at the fish in the baskets
you still bring home
I meet myself by the river
dropping tears like omens
to say good luck river
sail away stars
in that man sleeping
is a cave of gold!

IN THE QUIET THERE IS A DISTANCE

in my chest
a lotus is growing

in the dark as you are sleeping
I am half turned
to our neat row of jalousies
and despite the sounds of heels
clicking across the pavement
and the uncertain fate of mopeds
as they mosquito their way across our street
I feel myself uncoil, unfurl, and feel
a hard knot untwist and release
as unmarked as gardenias
that last so long without browning
as long as they are untouched

I let this moment come and go unannounced
and you have not sensed it
the shake of dew as the final leaf springs open
nor the sharp tug of my muscles
as the body moves as if to leave this place
as it yearns for comfort and what it thinks
that might be

I feel ready to go
inside, in lotus, in depth, in deep
moving as if through water

going inside myself
without exposure to the air
yet breathing
eyes open
not sleeping

you, sleeping
missing it all

SECTION THREE

ETHNOBOTANY

viewing *Morning Glory* by Sopheap Pich, 2011

I think about poems
and sometimes it's like that

genocide may be what the world is doing
but we try to feed ourselves and our children
words that gather like clouds of rice

accompanied by the skins of morning glories
we try to feel full on what we say
on what rises from the plate to our lips

THE ESSENTIAL NATURE OF THINGS

the essential nature of all things
is silence
the well we all drink from

the conduit for water
runs through everything
and changes into the pulse of electricity
from firefly
to lightning intermixed
with thunder

all of which is silence
moving

deliberate as glaciers
water creeps
in inches across the earth

LAND OF OBLIGATION

I
in the land of reciprocal obligation
the tongue and groove of hinges meet
made to be exact and equal

children test these thoughts
by pulling open a box of cigars
and fanning it like wings of a bird:
an awkward flying machine
with the smell of tobacco tumbling out

but the hinge stays steady
the spine of all things
the steel pin that holds open
the jaw of obligation

in the land of obligation, lovers know how far
they may stray off a path
or how much they can trust the coins in their pockets
or how deeply they may press against each other
or how loudly they may speak

knowing that their safety is not only held in their flesh
but is held too within the bones of their grandfather
or their mother
or the steam that rises above the cooking pot
they know the temporal nature of their lives
and that things tip easily in one direction or another

for like skin prone to bruising,

it is inevitable that they will be touched

but by what, they aren't sure, so they prepare
by planting stalks of obligation and harvesting them
like the ti leaves lei makers strip, wrap, and twist

into cords strong enough to bind them
to pull them out of unmade mortgage payments or layoffs
or bouts when one of them drinks too much
ropes laced and looped everywhere in their lives
enslaving them or securing them
this difference they may not know or want to discover
sleeping as they are in that place

I wake up in California
facing stop-lighted freeway on-ramps
self-serve counters in grocery chains
and buildings wrapped in miles of black plastic
that suddenly emerge pink and grotesque
on hillsides sheared off
and in their nakedness hold people
whose faces long to press against the cool glass
moved by the memory of the outside

I drift, suspended in this new world

like the astronaut who stayed twelve days in MIR
traveling 17,000 miles per hour
entering space with just one long tether
here, so easily, that last line to obligation
can be cut
hurling me though stars

opening great distances between me and all else
leaving no connection to the small earth
and its delicate systems below

II
my brother pushes a wheelbarrow full of gravel
while Ben and Casey bark
he struggles against it, and the soft hood of his sweatshirt
picks up the moisture of his skin and Hilo's airborne rain

in the land of obligation my brother is a victor
having paid his debts 17 years in service
for the defense
carrying those heavy books and the weight of lives
up tiny rickety stairs to some karmic counter of life

that spring he was inoperable, had a stroke,
was medevac'd
underwent brain surgery
and lost his speech along with the use of his left side
when he was half in the body and half in another world
they came to look in on him, to bring comfort,
to ask questions

there, some people may stand
and talk when they are happy.
when they are in grief, they are paralyzed
while others stand in hospital hallways,
big beefy men who aren't afraid to eat,
whose skin and melancholia are sometimes dark

they'll gently jostle each other as a way to joke;
they can feel their own hearts break
but can't quite say anything
and instead shake their heads
or nod without words when someone else comes by

with my brother, they stood in twos or threes
some in a great penetration of silence
others fluttering in with food that couldn't eaten
or flowers he couldn't smell
but the flood of all that
was something that his soul could ride on
so that even the nurses broke open
to a new level they hadn't before
letting him go down through the floors
while recovering from brain surgery
to see the dogs, the two yapping at him
in the hospital parking lot
their hearts having been broken too
the night that he fell motionless
the night Soo sat next to him
a woman who hates driving a car

flying in a helicopter
with people who couldn't explain medical terms
in a language she could speak

they flew
dark wings over all that water
while everyone waited below
stunned that such things could happen

III
my brother went into "arrest" five weeks after that
it's the first stage of remission

he still berates himself for not having left work earlier
to call his stepfather before he died
or for not sitting by his uncle's side when his soul left
taking whatever secrets or grief with him
swallowed up in that whorl of souls
stratifying themselves into the next life

but I like that he is home in Hilo
clocking his walks with birds
and their mele

terrible bird the helicopter that night.
beautiful bird having returned his soul to earth

in this land of reciprocity
chits are paid, breath is restored
an elixir is given from which the weary can drink:
a place where everything and nothing
get taken away

THE IDEAL MAN
    Chester Hideo Akamine
    (July 17, 1921 – March 18, 2008)
    Francis Paul Akamine
    (August 26, 1945 –March 7, 2010)

after viewing *The Ideal Man* exhibition at the
Metropolitan Art Museum
by prints curator Nadine Orenstein
I dream of my father
standing outside a wooden plantation-style house in Hilo
I confide in him and tell him how much I miss my brother

for the first time in my life
I lean on him
because the grieving force of water coming out of me
is more than I can bear

by now his chest and heart must be strong
as sure as the 4th century cuirass of bronze armor
that slides by me on exhibit
now softened by the green of age

the curator and my father
are strangers
yet equal
coming different distances
to comfort me
on this journey of grief

THIS TIME
    Patricia Ann (Akamine) Sasaki
    (February 19, 1950 - July 16, 2014)

you lose another
this time
your sister
and you think you can't recover
and you don't

not completely

but whatever gaps remain
she still fills

you sense her as you make decisions

you feel her as you drive
when you cut a corner too fast
you feel her make you hesitate
when you want to use a sharp word
as a blade

she's there in that space
that tender space
that only she can fill
and she fills it
fills it with air so you can breathe
with comfort so you feel free to cry

and if someone wounds you
she reminds you
they don't know who you are
then she rolls her eyes and you're free to laugh
even if your heart is breaking from missing her

missing her isn't possible because to do so
is to know with absolute certainty
that she's no longer there
which you cannot do

inside me is that ocean I tell myself
that I'm free to go
at anytime
and there I'm with her

there
I'm with her

I'm with her
every time

HĀPU`U

here at Volcano
the hāpu`u
take their time

they are slow growing
like the way they allow grieving

they grow as they choose
in the shades of green they choose
breathing in the vog
and the sulphured air
at home with the nature of rain
sometimes heavy and thudding
or sometimes the lightest mist that is barely seen
which makes a high gloss on everything

the mantles of its many names
like the Latin genus and species
have slid to the ground
unused by most
like all things that are uninvolved with the forest

things can be named
implying they are conquered
but only if they last on the lips
of the people who care about them

the hāpu`u curls or uncurls
reaching up to the sky
or dropping to the ground
in a cascade
it has its own course

it can't be commingled with the o`hia
which is living through its own quarantine

we were all so careless before
but now we know that everything affects everything
and that pathways can begin and end
with the absence
or presence of touch
or the absence or presence
of those we love

ACKNOWLEDGMENTS

Deep appreciation to family and friends who helped me through the many ups and downs during the time these poems were written.

Much gratitude also to Kumu Hula Kapena Malulani Perez and Kumu Hula Ann Lokeokaluapeleonālani Parker, whose joy and guidance kept me going when I had so many doubts.

And special thank you to Peter Nelson and to Delaina Thomas for all of the encouragement and support you both gave from the very beginning.

ABOUT THE AUTHOR

Pianta is a poet, fiction writer, and editor whose work has appeared in journals such as *Nimrod International Journal*, *Adirondack Review*, *Ekphrasis*, *Terrain.org*, and *Bamboo Ridge Press*, among others. Originally from O'ahu, she has lived in California and North Carolina but has returned to the Big Island of Hawai'i. Her readings often incorporate live music, dance, and multimedia. Her projects include a children's CD and songbook, *Little Bird: Songs for Children*, and a novella, *Old Volcano Road*. Her website can be found at www.pianta.org.

PUBLICATION CREDITS

"Mother," "Father," Nimrod International Journal, Fall 2019;"The Essential Nature of Things," "Ethnobotany," *San Diego Reader*, April 16, 2016; "Consolation" (formerly "Off the Coast,") *Bloodlotus*, No. 22, November 2011; "The Ideal Man," *Yuan Yang: A Journal of Hong Kong and International Writing*, 2011, Vol. 10, No. 1; "Second Consort: Jinzhan Yintai," "Second Consort: Spring Outing," *Ekphrasis*, Vol. 4 No. 6 Fall/Winter 2008; "Land of Obligation," *Bamboo Ridge: Journal of Hawai'i Literature and Arts*, No. 89, Spring 2006; "Atrium" (formerly "Sans Souci,"), "Reckless," *Bamboo Ridge: Journal of Hawai'i Literature and Arts*, No. 81, Spring 2002; Compass (formerly Inside There Is a Compass), *Bamboo Ridge: Journal of Hawai'i Literature and Arts*, No. 77, Spring 2000.

CURRENT RELEASES

Old Volcano Road
A novella
Ebook and print versions
Available on Kindle and Amazon

Little Bird: Songs for Children
CD of new, acoustic children's songs
Available on iTunes and Apple Music
Listen to samples at
https://pianta.hearnow.com/

Little Bird: Songs for Children Songbook
Accompanying songbook of lyrics and guitar chords
Available on Apple Books

Poetry
Hawai'i Poems: from there to here
Available at Apple Books

Before
Available on Apple Books

Acts and Intentions
Available on Amazon

Love and Grief in the Time of Ketu
Available on Amazon

Short Fiction
Floating
Available on Apple Books

For more information
www.pianta.org

www.ingramcontent.com/pod-product-compliance
Lightning Source LLC
Chambersburg PA
CBHW071408040426
42444CB00009B/2152